## ORDER LOGBOOK

| Name | |
|---|---|
| Logbook No. | |
| Start Date | |
| End Date | |

# ORDER

| Order No. | |
| Date | |

## CUSTOMER INFORMATION

| Name | |
| Company | |
| Phone No. | |
| Email | |

| Address | |

## ORDER DETAILS

| No. | Item Description | QTY | Price | Discount | Total |
|---|---|---|---|---|---|
| | | | | | |
| | | | | | |
| | | | | | |
| | | | | | |
| | | | | | |
| | | | | | |
| | | | | | |
| | | | | | |
| | | | | | |
| | | | | | |
| | | | | | |
| | | | | | |

| | Tax | |
|---|---|---|
| | Shipping | |
| | **TOTAL** | |

## ORDER STATUS

Started ☐   Completed ☐   Delivered ☐

## DELIVERY DETAILS

| Method | |
| Date | |
| Tracking No. | |
| Date Received | |

## NOTES

# ORDER

| Order No. | |
| --- | --- |
| Date | |

## CUSTOMER INFORMATION

| Name | | Address | |
| --- | --- | --- | --- |
| Company | | | |
| Phone No. | | | |
| Email | | | |

## ORDER DETAILS

| No. | Item Description | QTY | Price | Discount | Total |
| --- | --- | --- | --- | --- | --- |
| | | | | | |
| | | | | | |
| | | | | | |
| | | | | | |
| | | | | | |
| | | | | | |
| | | | | | |
| | | | | | |
| | | | | | |
| | | | | | |
| | | | | | |
| | | | | Tax | |

## ORDER STATUS

| | Shipping | |
| --- | --- | --- |
| Started ☐    Completed ☐    Delivered ☐ | **TOTAL** | |

## DELIVERY DETAILS

| Method | |
| --- | --- |
| Date | |
| Tracking No. | |
| Date Received | |

## NOTES

# ORDER

| Order No. | |
|---|---|
| Date | |

## CUSTOMER INFORMATION

| Name | |
|---|---|
| Company | |
| Phone No. | |
| Email | |

Address

## ORDER DETAILS

| No. | Item Description | QTY | Price | Discount | Total |
|---|---|---|---|---|---|
| | | | | | |
| | | | | | |
| | | | | | |
| | | | | | |
| | | | | | |
| | | | | | |
| | | | | | |
| | | | | | |
| | | | | | |
| | | | | | |
| | | | | | |

| | | |
|---|---|---|
| | Tax | |
| | Shipping | |
| | **TOTAL** | |

## ORDER STATUS

Started ☐   Completed ☐   Delivered ☐

## DELIVERY DETAILS

| Method | |
|---|---|
| Date | |
| Tracking No. | |
| Date Received | |

## NOTES

# ORDER

| Order No. | |
| Date | |

## CUSTOMER INFORMATION

| Name | |
| Company | |
| Phone No. | |
| Email | |

| Address | |

## ORDER DETAILS

| No. | Item Description | QTY | Price | Discount | Total |
|---|---|---|---|---|---|
| | | | | | |
| | | | | | |
| | | | | | |
| | | | | | |
| | | | | | |
| | | | | | |
| | | | | | |
| | | | | | |
| | | | | | |
| | | | | | |

## ORDER STATUS

Started ☐    Completed ☐    Delivered ☐

| Tax | |
| Shipping | |
| **TOTAL** | |

## DELIVERY DETAILS

| Method | |
| Date | |
| Tracking No. | |
| Date Received | |

## NOTES

# ORDER

| Order No. | |
|---|---|
| Date | |

## CUSTOMER INFORMATION

| Name | |
|---|---|
| Company | |
| Phone No. | |
| Email | |

| Address |
|---|
| |

## ORDER DETAILS

| No. | Item Description | QTY | Price | Discount | Total |
|---|---|---|---|---|---|
| | | | | | |
| | | | | | |
| | | | | | |
| | | | | | |
| | | | | | |
| | | | | | |
| | | | | | |
| | | | | | |
| | | | | | |
| | | | | | |
| | | | | | |

| | |
|---|---|
| Tax | |
| Shipping | |
| **TOTAL** | |

## ORDER STATUS

Started ☐    Completed ☐    Delivered ☐

## DELIVERY DETAILS

| Method | |
|---|---|
| Date | |
| Tracking No. | |
| Date Received | |

## NOTES

# ORDER

| Order No. | |
| --- | --- |
| Date | |

## CUSTOMER INFORMATION

| | | Address | |
| --- | --- | --- | --- |
| Name | | | |
| Company | | | |
| Phone No. | | | |
| Email | | | |

## ORDER DETAILS

| No. | Item Description | QTY | Price | Discount | Total |
| --- | --- | --- | --- | --- | --- |
| | | | | | |
| | | | | | |
| | | | | | |
| | | | | | |
| | | | | | |
| | | | | | |
| | | | | | |
| | | | | | |
| | | | | | |
| | | | | | |

## ORDER STATUS

Started ☐   Completed ☐   Delivered ☐

| Tax | |
| --- | --- |
| Shipping | |
| **TOTAL** | |

## DELIVERY DETAILS

| Method | |
| --- | --- |
| Date | |
| Tracking No. | |
| Date Received | |

## NOTES

# ORDER

Order No.

Date

## CUSTOMER INFORMATION

| Name |  |
|---|---|
| Company |  |
| Phone No. |  |
| Email |  |

Address

## ORDER DETAILS

| No. | Item Description | QTY | Price | Discount | Total |
|---|---|---|---|---|---|
|  |  |  |  |  |  |
|  |  |  |  |  |  |
|  |  |  |  |  |  |
|  |  |  |  |  |  |
|  |  |  |  |  |  |
|  |  |  |  |  |  |
|  |  |  |  |  |  |
|  |  |  |  |  |  |
|  |  |  |  |  |  |
|  |  |  |  |  |  |
|  |  |  |  |  |  |

| | Tax | |
|---|---|---|
| | Shipping | |
| | **TOTAL** | |

## ORDER STATUS

Started ☐   Completed ☐   Delivered ☐

## DELIVERY DETAILS

| Method |  |
|---|---|
| Date |  |
| Tracking No. |  |
| Date Received |  |

## NOTES

# ORDER

| Order No. | |
|---|---|
| Date | |

## CUSTOMER INFORMATION

| Name | | Address | |
|---|---|---|---|
| Company | | | |
| Phone No. | | | |
| Email | | | |

## ORDER DETAILS

| No. | Item Description | QTY | Price | Discount | Total |
|---|---|---|---|---|---|
| | | | | | |
| | | | | | |
| | | | | | |
| | | | | | |
| | | | | | |
| | | | | | |
| | | | | | |
| | | | | | |
| | | | | | |
| | | | | | |
| | | | | | |
| | | | | Tax | |
| | | | | Shipping | |

## ORDER STATUS

Started ☐     Completed ☐     Delivered ☐

**TOTAL**

## DELIVERY DETAILS

| Method | |
|---|---|
| Date | |
| Tracking No. | |
| Date Received | |

## NOTES

# ORDER

| Order No. | |
|---|---|
| Date | |

## CUSTOMER INFORMATION

| Name | |
|---|---|
| Company | |
| Phone No. | |
| Email | |

Address

## ORDER DETAILS

| No. | Item Description | QTY | Price | Discount | Total |
|---|---|---|---|---|---|
| | | | | | |
| | | | | | |
| | | | | | |
| | | | | | |
| | | | | | |
| | | | | | |
| | | | | | |
| | | | | | |
| | | | | | |
| | | | | | |
| | | | | | |
| | | | | | |

## ORDER STATUS

Started ☐  Completed ☐  Delivered ☐

| Tax | |
|---|---|
| Shipping | |
| **TOTAL** | |

## DELIVERY DETAILS

| Method | |
|---|---|
| Date | |
| Tracking No. | |
| Date Received | |

## NOTES

# ORDER

| Order No. | |
|---|---|
| Date | |

## CUSTOMER INFORMATION

| Name | | Address | |
|---|---|---|---|
| Company | | | |
| Phone No. | | | |
| Email | | | |

## ORDER DETAILS

| No. | Item Description | QTY | Price | Discount | Total |
|---|---|---|---|---|---|
| | | | | | |
| | | | | | |
| | | | | | |
| | | | | | |
| | | | | | |
| | | | | | |
| | | | | | |
| | | | | | |
| | | | | | |
| | | | | | |
| | | | | | |
| | | | | Tax | |
| | | | | Shipping | |
| | | | | **TOTAL** | |

## ORDER STATUS

Started ☐    Completed ☐    Delivered ☐

## DELIVERY DETAILS

| Method | |
|---|---|
| Date | |
| Tracking No. | |
| Date Received | |

## NOTES

# ORDER

| Order No. | |
|---|---|
| Date | |

## CUSTOMER INFORMATION

| | | | |
|---|---|---|---|
| Name | | Address | |
| Company | | | |
| Phone No. | | | |
| Email | | | |

## ORDER DETAILS

| No. | Item Description | QTY | Price | Discount | Total |
|---|---|---|---|---|---|
| | | | | | |
| | | | | | |
| | | | | | |
| | | | | | |
| | | | | | |
| | | | | | |
| | | | | | |
| | | | | | |
| | | | | | |
| | | | | | |
| | | | | Tax | |
| | | | | Shipping | |

## ORDER STATUS

Started ☐     Completed ☐     Delivered ☐

**TOTAL**

## DELIVERY DETAILS

| Method | |
|---|---|
| Date | |
| Tracking No. | |
| Date Received | |

## NOTES

# ORDER

| Order No. | |
| Date | |

## CUSTOMER INFORMATION

| Name | | Address | |
| Company | | | |
| Phone No. | | | |
| Email | | | |

## ORDER DETAILS

| No. | Item Description | QTY | Price | Discount | Total |
|---|---|---|---|---|---|
| | | | | | |
| | | | | | |
| | | | | | |
| | | | | | |
| | | | | | |
| | | | | | |
| | | | | | |
| | | | | | |
| | | | | | |
| | | | | | |
| | | | | | |
| | | | | | |
| | | | | | |

| | Tax | |
| **ORDER STATUS** | Shipping | |
| Started ☐  Completed ☐  Delivered ☐ | **TOTAL** | |

## DELIVERY DETAILS

| Method | |
| Date | |
| Tracking No. | |
| Date Received | |

## NOTES

# ORDER

| Order No. | |
| Date | |

## CUSTOMER INFORMATION

| Name | | Address | |
| Company | | | |
| Phone No. | | | |
| Email | | | |

## ORDER DETAILS

| No. | Item Description | QTY | Price | Discount | Total |
|---|---|---|---|---|---|
| | | | | | |
| | | | | | |
| | | | | | |
| | | | | | |
| | | | | | |
| | | | | | |
| | | | | | |
| | | | | | |
| | | | | | |
| | | | | | |
| | | | | | |

| | Tax | |
|---|---|---|
| **ORDER STATUS** | Shipping | |
| Started ☐   Completed ☐   Delivered ☐ | **TOTAL** | |

## DELIVERY DETAILS

| Method | |
| Date | |
| Tracking No. | |
| Date Received | |

## NOTES

# ORDER

| Order No. | |
|---|---|
| Date | |

## CUSTOMER INFORMATION

| Name | | Address | |
|---|---|---|---|
| Company | | | |
| Phone No. | | | |
| Email | | | |

## ORDER DETAILS

| No. | Item Description | QTY | Price | Discount | Total |
|---|---|---|---|---|---|
| | | | | | |
| | | | | | |
| | | | | | |
| | | | | | |
| | | | | | |
| | | | | | |
| | | | | | |
| | | | | | |
| | | | | | |
| | | | | | |
| | | | | | |

## ORDER STATUS

Started ☐    Completed ☐    Delivered ☐

| Tax | |
|---|---|
| Shipping | |
| **TOTAL** | |

## DELIVERY DETAILS

| Method | |
|---|---|
| Date | |
| Tracking No. | |
| Date Received | |

## NOTES

# ORDER

Order No.

Date

## CUSTOMER INFORMATION

| | |
|---|---|
| Name | |
| Company | |
| Phone No. | |
| Email | |

Address

## ORDER DETAILS

| No. | Item Description | QTY | Price | Discount | Total |
|---|---|---|---|---|---|
| | | | | | |
| | | | | | |
| | | | | | |
| | | | | | |
| | | | | | |
| | | | | | |
| | | | | | |
| | | | | | |
| | | | | | |
| | | | | | |
| | | | | | |
| | | | | | |

| | |
|---|---|
| Tax | |
| Shipping | |
| **TOTAL** | |

## ORDER STATUS

Started ☐    Completed ☐    Delivered ☐

## DELIVERY DETAILS

| | |
|---|---|
| Method | |
| Date | |
| Tracking No. | |
| Date Received | |

## NOTES

# ORDER

Order No.

Date

## CUSTOMER INFORMATION

| | |
|---|---|
| Name | |
| Company | |
| Phone No. | |
| Email | |

Address

## ORDER DETAILS

| No. | Item Description | QTY | Price | Discount | Total |
|---|---|---|---|---|---|
| | | | | | |
| | | | | | |
| | | | | | |
| | | | | | |
| | | | | | |
| | | | | | |
| | | | | | |
| | | | | | |
| | | | | | |
| | | | | | |
| | | | | | |

## ORDER STATUS

Started ☐   Completed ☐   Delivered ☐

Tax

Shipping

**TOTAL**

## DELIVERY DETAILS

| | |
|---|---|
| Method | |
| Date | |
| Tracking No. | |
| Date Received | |

## NOTES

# ORDER

| | |
|---|---|
| Order No. | |
| Date | |

## CUSTOMER INFORMATION

| | | | |
|---|---|---|---|
| Name | | Address | |
| Company | | | |
| Phone No. | | | |
| Email | | | |

## ORDER DETAILS

| No. | Item Description | QTY | Price | Discount | Total |
|---|---|---|---|---|---|
| | | | | | |
| | | | | | |
| | | | | | |
| | | | | | |
| | | | | | |
| | | | | | |
| | | | | | |
| | | | | | |
| | | | | | |
| | | | | | |
| | | | | | |
| | | | | Tax | |
| | | | | Shipping | |

## ORDER STATUS

Started ☐    Completed ☐    Delivered ☐    **TOTAL**

## DELIVERY DETAILS

| | |
|---|---|
| Method | |
| Date | |
| Tracking No. | |
| Date Received | |

## NOTES

# ORDER

| Order No. | |
|---|---|
| Date | |

## CUSTOMER INFORMATION

| Name | |
|---|---|
| Company | |
| Phone No. | |
| Email | |

Address

## ORDER DETAILS

| No. | Item Description | QTY | Price | Discount | Total |
|---|---|---|---|---|---|
| | | | | | |
| | | | | | |
| | | | | | |
| | | | | | |
| | | | | | |
| | | | | | |
| | | | | | |
| | | | | | |
| | | | | | |
| | | | | | |
| | | | | | |

## ORDER STATUS

Started ☐    Completed ☐    Delivered ☐

| Tax | |
|---|---|
| Shipping | |
| **TOTAL** | |

## DELIVERY DETAILS

| Method | |
|---|---|
| Date | |
| Tracking No. | |
| Date Received | |

## NOTES

# ORDER

| | |
|---|---|
| Order No. | |
| Date | |

## CUSTOMER INFORMATION

| | |
|---|---|
| Name | |
| Company | |
| Phone No. | |
| Email | |

**Address**

## ORDER DETAILS

| No. | Item Description | QTY | Price | Discount | Total |
|---|---|---|---|---|---|
| | | | | | |
| | | | | | |
| | | | | | |
| | | | | | |
| | | | | | |
| | | | | | |
| | | | | | |
| | | | | | |
| | | | | | |
| | | | | | |
| | | | | | |

| | |
|---|---|
| Tax | |
| Shipping | |
| **TOTAL** | |

## ORDER STATUS

Started ☐   Completed ☐   Delivered ☐

## DELIVERY DETAILS

| | |
|---|---|
| Method | |
| Date | |
| Tracking No. | |
| Date Received | |

## NOTES

# ORDER

| Order No. | |
| Date | |

## CUSTOMER INFORMATION

| Name | |
| Company | |
| Phone No. | |
| Email | |

| Address | |

## ORDER DETAILS

| No. | Item Description | QTY | Price | Discount | Total |
|---|---|---|---|---|---|
| | | | | | |
| | | | | | |
| | | | | | |
| | | | | | |
| | | | | | |
| | | | | | |
| | | | | | |
| | | | | | |
| | | | | | |
| | | | | | |

| | Tax | |
| | Shipping | |
| | **TOTAL** | |

## ORDER STATUS

Started ☐     Completed ☐     Delivered ☐

## DELIVERY DETAILS

| Method | |
| Date | |
| Tracking No. | |
| Date Received | |

## NOTES

# ORDER

| Order No. | |
| Date | |

## CUSTOMER INFORMATION

| Name | | Address | |
| Company | | | |
| Phone No. | | | |
| Email | | | |

## ORDER DETAILS

| No. | Item Description | QTY | Price | Discount | Total |
|---|---|---|---|---|---|
| | | | | | |
| | | | | | |
| | | | | | |
| | | | | | |
| | | | | | |
| | | | | | |
| | | | | | |
| | | | | | |
| | | | | | |
| | | | | | |
| | | | | | |
| | | | | Tax | |
| | | | | Shipping | |

## ORDER STATUS

Started ☐   Completed ☐   Delivered ☐

| | | | | **TOTAL** | |

## DELIVERY DETAILS

| Method | |
| Date | |
| Tracking No. | |
| Date Received | |

## NOTES

# ORDER

| Order No. | |
|---|---|
| Date | |

## CUSTOMER INFORMATION

| Name | | Address | |
|---|---|---|---|
| Company | | | |
| Phone No. | | | |
| Email | | | |

## ORDER DETAILS

| No. | Item Description | QTY | Price | Discount | Total |
|---|---|---|---|---|---|
| | | | | | |
| | | | | | |
| | | | | | |
| | | | | | |
| | | | | | |
| | | | | | |
| | | | | | |
| | | | | | |
| | | | | | |
| | | | | | |
| | | | | | |
| | | | | Tax | |
| | | | | Shipping | |

### ORDER STATUS

Started ☐    Completed ☐    Delivered ☐

**TOTAL**

## DELIVERY DETAILS

| Method | |
|---|---|
| Date | |
| Tracking No. | |
| Date Received | |

## NOTES

# ORDER

| Order No. | |
|---|---|
| Date | |

## CUSTOMER INFORMATION

| Name | |
|---|---|
| Company | |
| Phone No. | |
| Email | |

| Address |
|---|
| |

## ORDER DETAILS

| No. | Item Description | QTY | Price | Discount | Total |
|---|---|---|---|---|---|
| | | | | | |
| | | | | | |
| | | | | | |
| | | | | | |
| | | | | | |
| | | | | | |
| | | | | | |
| | | | | | |
| | | | | | |
| | | | | | |
| | | | | | |
| | | | | | |

| Tax | |
|---|---|
| Shipping | |
| **TOTAL** | |

## ORDER STATUS

Started ☐    Completed ☐    Delivered ☐

## DELIVERY DETAILS

| Method | |
|---|---|
| Date | |
| Tracking No. | |
| Date Received | |

## NOTES

# ORDER

Order No.

Date

## CUSTOMER INFORMATION

| | | |
|---|---|---|
| Name | | Address |
| Company | | |
| Phone No. | | |
| Email | | |

## ORDER DETAILS

| No. | Item Description | QTY | Price | Discount | Total |
|---|---|---|---|---|---|
| | | | | | |
| | | | | | |
| | | | | | |
| | | | | | |
| | | | | | |
| | | | | | |
| | | | | | |
| | | | | | |
| | | | | | |
| | | | | | |

| | | |
|---|---|---|
| | | Tax |
| | | Shipping |
| | | **TOTAL** |

## ORDER STATUS

Started ☐   Completed ☐   Delivered ☐

## DELIVERY DETAILS

| | |
|---|---|
| Method | |
| Date | |
| Tracking No. | |
| Date Received | |

## NOTES

# ORDER

| Order No. | |
|---|---|
| Date | |

## CUSTOMER INFORMATION

| | | Address | |
|---|---|---|---|
| Name | | | |
| Company | | | |
| Phone No. | | | |
| Email | | | |

## ORDER DETAILS

| No. | Item Description | QTY | Price | Discount | Total |
|---|---|---|---|---|---|
| | | | | | |
| | | | | | |
| | | | | | |
| | | | | | |
| | | | | | |
| | | | | | |
| | | | | | |
| | | | | | |
| | | | | | |
| | | | | | |
| | | | | Tax | |
| | | | | Shipping | |

## ORDER STATUS

Started ☐   Completed ☐   Delivered ☐   **TOTAL**

## DELIVERY DETAILS

| Method | |
|---|---|
| Date | |
| Tracking No. | |
| Date Received | |

## NOTES

# ORDER

| | |
|---|---|
| Order No. | |
| Date | |

## CUSTOMER INFORMATION

| | | | |
|---|---|---|---|
| Name | | Address | |
| Company | | | |
| Phone No. | | | |
| Email | | | |

## ORDER DETAILS

| No. | Item Description | QTY | Price | Discount | Total |
|---|---|---|---|---|---|
| | | | | | |
| | | | | | |
| | | | | | |
| | | | | | |
| | | | | | |
| | | | | | |
| | | | | | |
| | | | | | |
| | | | | | |
| | | | | | |
| | | | | | |
| | | | | Tax | |
| | | | | Shipping | |

## ORDER STATUS

Started ☐   Completed ☐   Delivered ☐

**TOTAL**

## DELIVERY DETAILS

| | |
|---|---|
| Method | |
| Date | |
| Tracking No. | |
| Date Received | |

## NOTES

# ORDER

| Order No. | |
| Date | |

## CUSTOMER INFORMATION

| Name | |
|---|---|
| Company | |
| Phone No. | |
| Email | |

| Address | |
|---|---|

## ORDER DETAILS

| No. | Item Description | QTY | Price | Discount | Total |
|---|---|---|---|---|---|
| | | | | | |
| | | | | | |
| | | | | | |
| | | | | | |
| | | | | | |
| | | | | | |
| | | | | | |
| | | | | | |
| | | | | | |
| | | | | | |
| | | | | | |

| | |
|---|---|
| Tax | |
| Shipping | |
| **TOTAL** | |

## ORDER STATUS

Started ☐    Completed ☐    Delivered ☐

## DELIVERY DETAILS

| Method | |
|---|---|
| Date | |
| Tracking No. | |
| Date Received | |

## NOTES

# ORDER

Order No.
Date

## CUSTOMER INFORMATION

| | |
|---|---|
| Name | |
| Company | |
| Phone No. | |
| Email | |

Address

## ORDER DETAILS

| No. | Item Description | QTY | Price | Discount | Total |
|---|---|---|---|---|---|
| | | | | | |
| | | | | | |
| | | | | | |
| | | | | | |
| | | | | | |
| | | | | | |
| | | | | | |
| | | | | | |
| | | | | | |
| | | | | | |
| | | | | | |

| | |
|---|---|
| Tax | |
| Shipping | |
| **TOTAL** | |

## ORDER STATUS

Started ☐  Completed ☐  Delivered ☐

## DELIVERY DETAILS

| | |
|---|---|
| Method | |
| Date | |
| Tracking No. | |
| Date Received | |

## NOTES

# ORDER

| | |
|---|---|
| Order No. | |
| Date | |

## CUSTOMER INFORMATION

| | | | |
|---|---|---|---|
| Name | | Address | |
| Company | | | |
| Phone No. | | | |
| Email | | | |

## ORDER DETAILS

| No. | Item Description | QTY | Price | Discount | Total |
|---|---|---|---|---|---|
| | | | | | |
| | | | | | |
| | | | | | |
| | | | | | |
| | | | | | |
| | | | | | |
| | | | | | |
| | | | | | |
| | | | | | |
| | | | | | |
| | | | | | |
| | | | | Tax | |
| | | | | Shipping | |

## ORDER STATUS

Started ☐    Completed ☐    Delivered ☐

**TOTAL**

## DELIVERY DETAILS

| | |
|---|---|
| Method | |
| Date | |
| Tracking No. | |
| Date Received | |

## NOTES

# ORDER

| Order No. | |
|---|---|
| Date | |

## CUSTOMER INFORMATION

| Name | | Address | |
|---|---|---|---|
| Company | | | |
| Phone No. | | | |
| Email | | | |

## ORDER DETAILS

| No. | Item Description | QTY | Price | Discount | Total |
|---|---|---|---|---|---|
| | | | | | |
| | | | | | |
| | | | | | |
| | | | | | |
| | | | | | |
| | | | | | |
| | | | | | |
| | | | | | |
| | | | | | |
| | | | | | |
| | | | | | |
| | | | | Tax | |
| | | | | Shipping | |

## ORDER STATUS

Started ☐   Completed ☐   Delivered ☐

**TOTAL**

## DELIVERY DETAILS

| Method | |
|---|---|
| Date | |
| Tracking No. | |
| Date Received | |

## NOTES

# ORDER

| Order No. | |
| Date | |

## CUSTOMER INFORMATION

| Name | | Address | |
| Company | | | |
| Phone No. | | | |
| Email | | | |

## ORDER DETAILS

| No. | Item Description | QTY | Price | Discount | Total |
|---|---|---|---|---|---|
| | | | | | |
| | | | | | |
| | | | | | |
| | | | | | |
| | | | | | |
| | | | | | |
| | | | | | |
| | | | | | |
| | | | | | |
| | | | | | |
| | | | | | |

## ORDER STATUS

Started ☐   Completed ☐   Delivered ☐

| Tax | |
| Shipping | |
| **TOTAL** | |

## DELIVERY DETAILS

| Method | |
| Date | |
| Tracking No. | |
| Date Received | |

## NOTES

# ORDER

| Order No. | |
| Date | |

## CUSTOMER INFORMATION

| Name | | Address | |
| Company | | | |
| Phone No. | | | |
| Email | | | |

## ORDER DETAILS

| No. | Item Description | QTY | Price | Discount | Total |
|---|---|---|---|---|---|
| | | | | | |
| | | | | | |
| | | | | | |
| | | | | | |
| | | | | | |
| | | | | | |
| | | | | | |
| | | | | | |
| | | | | | |
| | | | | | |
| | | | | | |
| | | | | Tax | |
| | | | | Shipping | |

### ORDER STATUS

Started ☐    Completed ☐    Delivered ☐

**TOTAL**

## DELIVERY DETAILS

| Method | |
| Date | |
| Tracking No. | |
| Date Received | |

## NOTES

# ORDER

| Order No. | |
| Date | |

## CUSTOMER INFORMATION

| Name | |
|---|---|
| Company | |
| Phone No. | |
| Email | |

| Address | |
|---|---|
| | |

## ORDER DETAILS

| No. | Item Description | QTY | Price | Discount | Total |
|---|---|---|---|---|---|
| | | | | | |
| | | | | | |
| | | | | | |
| | | | | | |
| | | | | | |
| | | | | | |
| | | | | | |
| | | | | | |
| | | | | | |
| | | | | | |
| | | | | | |

| | Tax | |
|---|---|---|
| | Shipping | |
| | **TOTAL** | |

## ORDER STATUS

Started ☐     Completed ☐     Delivered ☐

## DELIVERY DETAILS

| Method | |
|---|---|
| Date | |
| Tracking No. | |
| Date Received | |

## NOTES

# ORDER

| Order No. | |
|---|---|
| Date | |

## CUSTOMER INFORMATION

| Name | | Address | |
|---|---|---|---|
| Company | | | |
| Phone No. | | | |
| Email | | | |

## ORDER DETAILS

| No. | Item Description | QTY | Price | Discount | Total |
|---|---|---|---|---|---|
| | | | | | |
| | | | | | |
| | | | | | |
| | | | | | |
| | | | | | |
| | | | | | |
| | | | | | |
| | | | | | |
| | | | | | |
| | | | | | |
| | | | | | |

| | Tax | |
|---|---|---|
| **ORDER STATUS** | Shipping | |
| Started ☐  Completed ☐  Delivered ☐ | **TOTAL** | |

## DELIVERY DETAILS

| Method | |
|---|---|
| Date | |
| Tracking No. | |
| Date Received | |

## NOTES

# ORDER

Order No.

Date

## CUSTOMER INFORMATION

| | |
|---|---|
| Name | |
| Company | |
| Phone No. | |
| Email | |

Address

## ORDER DETAILS

| No. | Item Description | QTY | Price | Discount | Total |
|---|---|---|---|---|---|
| | | | | | |
| | | | | | |
| | | | | | |
| | | | | | |
| | | | | | |
| | | | | | |
| | | | | | |
| | | | | | |
| | | | | | |
| | | | | | |

| | |
|---|---|
| Tax | |
| Shipping | |
| **TOTAL** | |

## ORDER STATUS

Started ☐    Completed ☐    Delivered ☐

## DELIVERY DETAILS

| | |
|---|---|
| Method | |
| Date | |
| Tracking No. | |
| Date Received | |

## NOTES

# ORDER

Order No.

Date

## CUSTOMER INFORMATION

| | |
|---|---|
| Name | |
| Company | |
| Phone No. | |
| Email | |

Address

## ORDER DETAILS

| No. | Item Description | QTY | Price | Discount | Total |
|---|---|---|---|---|---|
| | | | | | |
| | | | | | |
| | | | | | |
| | | | | | |
| | | | | | |
| | | | | | |
| | | | | | |
| | | | | | |
| | | | | | |
| | | | | | |
| | | | | | |
| | | | | Tax | |
| | | | | Shipping | |
| | | | | **TOTAL** | |

## ORDER STATUS

Started ☐     Completed ☐     Delivered ☐

## DELIVERY DETAILS

| | |
|---|---|
| Method | |
| Date | |
| Tracking No. | |
| Date Received | |

## NOTES

# ORDER

| Order No. | |
| Date | |

## CUSTOMER INFORMATION

| Name | | Address | |
| Company | | | |
| Phone No. | | | |
| Email | | | |

## ORDER DETAILS

| No. | Item Description | QTY | Price | Discount | Total |
|-----|------------------|-----|-------|----------|-------|
|     |                  |     |       |          |       |
|     |                  |     |       |          |       |
|     |                  |     |       |          |       |
|     |                  |     |       |          |       |
|     |                  |     |       |          |       |
|     |                  |     |       |          |       |
|     |                  |     |       |          |       |
|     |                  |     |       |          |       |
|     |                  |     |       |          |       |
|     |                  |     |       |          |       |
|     |                  |     |       |          |       |

| | Tax | |
| | Shipping | |
| | **TOTAL** | |

## ORDER STATUS

Started ☐    Completed ☐    Delivered ☐

## DELIVERY DETAILS

| Method | |
| Date | |
| Tracking No. | |
| Date Received | |

## NOTES

# ORDER

| Order No. | |
|---|---|
| Date | |

## CUSTOMER INFORMATION

| Name | | Address | |
|---|---|---|---|
| Company | | | |
| Phone No. | | | |
| Email | | | |

## ORDER DETAILS

| No. | Item Description | QTY | Price | Discount | Total |
|---|---|---|---|---|---|
| | | | | | |
| | | | | | |
| | | | | | |
| | | | | | |
| | | | | | |
| | | | | | |
| | | | | | |
| | | | | | |
| | | | | | |
| | | | | | |
| | | | | | |
| | | | | | |

## ORDER STATUS

Started ☐    Completed ☐    Delivered ☐

| Tax | |
|---|---|
| Shipping | |
| **TOTAL** | |

## DELIVERY DETAILS

| Method | |
|---|---|
| Date | |
| Tracking No. | |
| Date Received | |

## NOTES

# ORDER

| Order No. | |
| Date | |

## CUSTOMER INFORMATION

| Name | | Address | |
|---|---|---|---|
| Company | | | |
| Phone No. | | | |
| Email | | | |

## ORDER DETAILS

| No. | Item Description | QTY | Price | Discount | Total |
|---|---|---|---|---|---|
| | | | | | |
| | | | | | |
| | | | | | |
| | | | | | |
| | | | | | |
| | | | | | |
| | | | | | |
| | | | | | |
| | | | | | |
| | | | | | |
| | | | | | |
| | | | | Tax | |
| | | | | Shipping | |
| | | | | **TOTAL** | |

## ORDER STATUS

Started ☐    Completed ☐    Delivered ☐

## DELIVERY DETAILS

| Method | |
|---|---|
| Date | |
| Tracking No. | |
| Date Received | |

## NOTES

# ORDER

| Order No. | |
|---|---|
| Date | |

## CUSTOMER INFORMATION

| Name | | Address | |
|---|---|---|---|
| Company | | | |
| Phone No. | | | |
| Email | | | |

## ORDER DETAILS

| No. | Item Description | QTY | Price | Discount | Total |
|---|---|---|---|---|---|
| | | | | | |
| | | | | | |
| | | | | | |
| | | | | | |
| | | | | | |
| | | | | | |
| | | | | | |
| | | | | | |
| | | | | | |
| | | | | | |

## ORDER STATUS

Started ☐     Completed ☐     Delivered ☐

| | |
|---|---|
| Tax | |
| Shipping | |
| **TOTAL** | |

## DELIVERY DETAILS

| Method | |
|---|---|
| Date | |
| Tracking No. | |
| Date Received | |

## NOTES

# ORDER

Order No.

Date

## CUSTOMER INFORMATION

| Name | | Address | |
|---|---|---|---|
| Company | | | |
| Phone No. | | | |
| Email | | | |

## ORDER DETAILS

| No. | Item Description | QTY | Price | Discount | Total |
|---|---|---|---|---|---|
| | | | | | |
| | | | | | |
| | | | | | |
| | | | | | |
| | | | | | |
| | | | | | |
| | | | | | |
| | | | | | |
| | | | | | |
| | | | | | |
| | | | | | |

## ORDER STATUS

Started ☐    Completed ☐    Delivered ☐

Tax
Shipping
**TOTAL**

## DELIVERY DETAILS

| Method | |
|---|---|
| Date | |
| Tracking No. | |
| Date Received | |

## NOTES

# ORDER

| Order No. | |
|---|---|
| Date | |

## CUSTOMER INFORMATION

| Name | |
|---|---|
| Company | |
| Phone No. | |
| Email | |

Address

## ORDER DETAILS

| No. | Item Description | QTY | Price | Discount | Total |
|---|---|---|---|---|---|
| | | | | | |
| | | | | | |
| | | | | | |
| | | | | | |
| | | | | | |
| | | | | | |
| | | | | | |
| | | | | | |
| | | | | | |
| | | | | | |

## ORDER STATUS

Started ☐   Completed ☐   Delivered ☐

| Tax | |
|---|---|
| Shipping | |
| **TOTAL** | |

## DELIVERY DETAILS

| Method | |
|---|---|
| Date | |
| Tracking No. | |
| Date Received | |

## NOTES

# ORDER

Order No.

Date

## CUSTOMER INFORMATION

| Name |
|---|
| Company |
| Phone No. |
| Email |

Address

## ORDER DETAILS

| No. | Item Description | QTY | Price | Discount | Total |
|---|---|---|---|---|---|
| | | | | | |
| | | | | | |
| | | | | | |
| | | | | | |
| | | | | | |
| | | | | | |
| | | | | | |
| | | | | | |
| | | | | | |
| | | | | | |
| | | | | | |

Tax

Shipping

**TOTAL**

## ORDER STATUS

Started ☐     Completed ☐     Delivered ☐

## DELIVERY DETAILS

| Method |
|---|
| Date |
| Tracking No. |
| Date Received |

## NOTES

# ORDER

| Order No. | |
| Date | |

## CUSTOMER INFORMATION

| Name | | Address | |
| Company | | | |
| Phone No. | | | |
| Email | | | |

## ORDER DETAILS

| No. | Item Description | QTY | Price | Discount | Total |
|---|---|---|---|---|---|
| | | | | | |
| | | | | | |
| | | | | | |
| | | | | | |
| | | | | | |
| | | | | | |
| | | | | | |
| | | | | | |
| | | | | | |
| | | | | | |
| | | | | | |
| | | | | | |

## ORDER STATUS

Started ☐     Completed ☐     Delivered ☐

| Tax | |
| Shipping | |
| **TOTAL** | |

## DELIVERY DETAILS

| Method | |
| Date | |
| Tracking No. | |
| Date Received | |

## NOTES

# ORDER

| Order No. | |
| Date | |

## CUSTOMER INFORMATION

| Name | | Address | |
| Company | | | |
| Phone No. | | | |
| Email | | | |

## ORDER DETAILS

| No. | Item Description | QTY | Price | Discount | Total |
|---|---|---|---|---|---|
| | | | | | |
| | | | | | |
| | | | | | |
| | | | | | |
| | | | | | |
| | | | | | |
| | | | | | |
| | | | | | |
| | | | | | |
| | | | | | |
| | | | | | |

## ORDER STATUS

Started ☐   Completed ☐   Delivered ☐

| Tax | |
| Shipping | |
| **TOTAL** | |

## DELIVERY DETAILS

| Method | |
| Date | |
| Tracking No. | |
| Date Received | |

## NOTES

# ORDER

| Order No. | |
|---|---|
| Date | |

## CUSTOMER INFORMATION

| Name | |
|---|---|
| Company | |
| Phone No. | |
| Email | |

Address

## ORDER DETAILS

| No. | Item Description | QTY | Price | Discount | Total |
|---|---|---|---|---|---|
| | | | | | |
| | | | | | |
| | | | | | |
| | | | | | |
| | | | | | |
| | | | | | |
| | | | | | |
| | | | | | |
| | | | | | |
| | | | | | |
| | | | | | |

### ORDER STATUS

Started ☐   Completed ☐   Delivered ☐

| Tax | |
|---|---|
| Shipping | |
| **TOTAL** | |

## DELIVERY DETAILS

| Method | |
|---|---|
| Date | |
| Tracking No. | |
| Date Received | |

## NOTES

# ORDER

| Order No. | |
| Date | |

## CUSTOMER INFORMATION

| Name | | Address | |
|---|---|---|---|
| Company | | | |
| Phone No. | | | |
| Email | | | |

## ORDER DETAILS

| No. | Item Description | QTY | Price | Discount | Total |
|---|---|---|---|---|---|
| | | | | | |
| | | | | | |
| | | | | | |
| | | | | | |
| | | | | | |
| | | | | | |
| | | | | | |
| | | | | | |
| | | | | | |
| | | | | | |
| | | | | | |
| | | | | Tax | |
| | | | | Shipping | |

## ORDER STATUS

Started ☐   Completed ☐   Delivered ☐

**TOTAL**

## DELIVERY DETAILS

| Method | |
|---|---|
| Date | |
| Tracking No. | |
| Date Received | |

## NOTES

# ORDER

| Order No. | |
| Date | |

## CUSTOMER INFORMATION

| Name | | Address | |
| Company | | | |
| Phone No. | | | |
| Email | | | |

## ORDER DETAILS

| No. | Item Description | QTY | Price | Discount | Total |
|---|---|---|---|---|---|
| | | | | | |
| | | | | | |
| | | | | | |
| | | | | | |
| | | | | | |
| | | | | | |
| | | | | | |
| | | | | | |
| | | | | | |
| | | | | | |
| | | | | | |
| | | | | | Tax |
| | | | | | Shipping |

## ORDER STATUS

Started ☐    Completed ☐    Delivered ☐

**TOTAL**

## DELIVERY DETAILS

| Method | |
| Date | |
| Tracking No. | |
| Date Received | |

## NOTES

# ORDER

| Order No. | |
| Date | |

## CUSTOMER INFORMATION

| Name | | Address | |
| Company | | | |
| Phone No. | | | |
| Email | | | |

## ORDER DETAILS

| No. | Item Description | QTY | Price | Discount | Total |
|---|---|---|---|---|---|
| | | | | | |
| | | | | | |
| | | | | | |
| | | | | | |
| | | | | | |
| | | | | | |
| | | | | | |
| | | | | | |
| | | | | | |
| | | | | | |
| | | | | | |

| | Tax | |
| ## ORDER STATUS | Shipping | |
| | **TOTAL** | |

Started ☐    Completed ☐    Delivered ☐

## DELIVERY DETAILS

| Method | |
| Date | |
| Tracking No. | |
| Date Received | |

## NOTES

# ORDER

| Order No. | |
| Date | |

## CUSTOMER INFORMATION

| Name | |
| Company | |
| Phone No. | |
| Email | |

Address

## ORDER DETAILS

| No. | Item Description | QTY | Price | Discount | Total |
|---|---|---|---|---|---|
| | | | | | |
| | | | | | |
| | | | | | |
| | | | | | |
| | | | | | |
| | | | | | |
| | | | | | |
| | | | | | |
| | | | | | |
| | | | | | |

## ORDER STATUS

Started ☐    Completed ☐    Delivered ☐

| Tax | |
| Shipping | |
| **TOTAL** | |

## DELIVERY DETAILS

| Method | |
| Date | |
| Tracking No. | |
| Date Received | |

## NOTES

# ORDER

| Order No. | |
| Date | |

## CUSTOMER INFORMATION

| Name | |
|---|---|
| Company | |
| Phone No. | |
| Email | |

| Address | |
|---|---|

## ORDER DETAILS

| No. | Item Description | QTY | Price | Discount | Total |
|---|---|---|---|---|---|
| | | | | | |
| | | | | | |
| | | | | | |
| | | | | | |
| | | | | | |
| | | | | | |
| | | | | | |
| | | | | | |
| | | | | | |
| | | | | | |
| | | | | | |

| | Tax | |
|---|---|---|
| | Shipping | |
| | **TOTAL** | |

## ORDER STATUS

Started ☐    Completed ☐    Delivered ☐

## DELIVERY DETAILS

| Method | |
|---|---|
| Date | |
| Tracking No. | |
| Date Received | |

## NOTES

# ORDER

| | |
|---|---|
| Order No. | |
| Date | |

## CUSTOMER INFORMATION

| | | | |
|---|---|---|---|
| Name | | Address | |
| Company | | | |
| Phone No. | | | |
| Email | | | |

## ORDER DETAILS

| No. | Item Description | QTY | Price | Discount | Total |
|---|---|---|---|---|---|
| | | | | | |
| | | | | | |
| | | | | | |
| | | | | | |
| | | | | | |
| | | | | | |
| | | | | | |
| | | | | | |
| | | | | | |
| | | | | | |

|  |  |
|---|---|
| Tax | |
| Shipping | |
| **TOTAL** | |

### ORDER STATUS

Started ☐    Completed ☐    Delivered ☐

## DELIVERY DETAILS

| | |
|---|---|
| Method | |
| Date | |
| Tracking No. | |
| Date Received | |

## NOTES

# ORDER

Order No.

Date

## CUSTOMER INFORMATION

| Name | | Address |
|---|---|---|
| Company | | |
| Phone No. | | |
| Email | | |

## ORDER DETAILS

| No. | Item Description | QTY | Price | Discount | Total |
|---|---|---|---|---|---|
| | | | | | |
| | | | | | |
| | | | | | |
| | | | | | |
| | | | | | |
| | | | | | |
| | | | | | |
| | | | | | |
| | | | | | |
| | | | | | |
| | | | | | |
| | | | | | |

|  |  |
|---|---|
| Tax | |
| Shipping | |
| **TOTAL** | |

## ORDER STATUS

Started ☐   Completed ☐   Delivered ☐

## DELIVERY DETAILS

| Method | |
|---|---|
| Date | |
| Tracking No. | |
| Date Received | |

## NOTES

# ORDER

| Order No. | |
|---|---|
| Date | |

## CUSTOMER INFORMATION

| Name | |
|---|---|
| Company | |
| Phone No. | |
| Email | |

| Address | |
|---|---|

## ORDER DETAILS

| No. | Item Description | QTY | Price | Discount | Total |
|---|---|---|---|---|---|
| | | | | | |
| | | | | | |
| | | | | | |
| | | | | | |
| | | | | | |
| | | | | | |
| | | | | | |
| | | | | | |
| | | | | | |
| | | | | | |

### ORDER STATUS

Started ☐    Completed ☐    Delivered ☐

| Tax | |
|---|---|
| Shipping | |
| **TOTAL** | |

## DELIVERY DETAILS

| Method | |
|---|---|
| Date | |
| Tracking No. | |
| Date Received | |

## NOTES

# ORDER

| Order No. | |
|---|---|
| Date | |

## CUSTOMER INFORMATION

| Name | |
|---|---|
| Company | |
| Phone No. | |
| Email | |

| Address |
|---|
| |

## ORDER DETAILS

| No. | Item Description | QTY | Price | Discount | Total |
|---|---|---|---|---|---|
| | | | | | |
| | | | | | |
| | | | | | |
| | | | | | |
| | | | | | |
| | | | | | |
| | | | | | |
| | | | | | |
| | | | | | |
| | | | | | |
| | | | | | |
| | | | | Tax | |
| | | | | Shipping | |

## ORDER STATUS

Started ☐   Completed ☐   Delivered ☐

**TOTAL**

## DELIVERY DETAILS

| Method | |
|---|---|
| Date | |
| Tracking No. | |
| Date Received | |

## NOTES

# ORDER

| Order No. | |
| Date | |

## CUSTOMER INFORMATION

| Name | |
|---|---|
| Company | |
| Phone No. | |
| Email | |

Address

## ORDER DETAILS

| No. | Item Description | QTY | Price | Discount | Total |
|---|---|---|---|---|---|
| | | | | | |
| | | | | | |
| | | | | | |
| | | | | | |
| | | | | | |
| | | | | | |
| | | | | | |
| | | | | | |
| | | | | | |
| | | | | | |
| | | | | | |
| | | | | | |

## ORDER STATUS

Started ☐  Completed ☐  Delivered ☐

| Tax | |
|---|---|
| Shipping | |
| **TOTAL** | |

## DELIVERY DETAILS

| Method | |
|---|---|
| Date | |
| Tracking No. | |
| Date Received | |

## NOTES

# ORDER

| Order No. | |
| Date | |

## CUSTOMER INFORMATION

| Name | | Address | |
| Company | | | |
| Phone No. | | | |
| Email | | | |

## ORDER DETAILS

| No. | Item Description | QTY | Price | Discount | Total |
|---|---|---|---|---|---|
| | | | | | |
| | | | | | |
| | | | | | |
| | | | | | |
| | | | | | |
| | | | | | |
| | | | | | |
| | | | | | |
| | | | | | |
| | | | | | |

### ORDER STATUS

Started ☐     Completed ☐     Delivered ☐

| Tax | |
| Shipping | |
| **TOTAL** | |

## DELIVERY DETAILS

| Method | |
| Date | |
| Tracking No. | |
| Date Received | |

## NOTES

# ORDER

| Order No. | |
| Date | |

## CUSTOMER INFORMATION

| Name | |
|---|---|
| Company | |
| Phone No. | |
| Email | |

| Address |
|---|
| |

## ORDER DETAILS

| No. | Item Description | QTY | Price | Discount | Total |
|---|---|---|---|---|---|
| | | | | | |
| | | | | | |
| | | | | | |
| | | | | | |
| | | | | | |
| | | | | | |
| | | | | | |
| | | | | | |
| | | | | | |
| | | | | | |

| Tax | |
|---|---|
| Shipping | |
| **TOTAL** | |

## ORDER STATUS

Started ☐    Completed ☐    Delivered ☐

## DELIVERY DETAILS

| Method | |
|---|---|
| Date | |
| Tracking No. | |
| Date Received | |

## NOTES

# ORDER

| Order No. | |
|---|---|
| Date | |

## CUSTOMER INFORMATION

| | | Address | |
|---|---|---|---|
| Name | | | |
| Company | | | |
| Phone No. | | | |
| Email | | | |

## ORDER DETAILS

| No. | Item Description | QTY | Price | Discount | Total |
|---|---|---|---|---|---|
| | | | | | |
| | | | | | |
| | | | | | |
| | | | | | |
| | | | | | |
| | | | | | |
| | | | | | |
| | | | | | |
| | | | | | |
| | | | | Tax | |
| | | | | Shipping | |

## ORDER STATUS

Started ☐   Completed ☐   Delivered ☐   **TOTAL**

## DELIVERY DETAILS

| Method | |
|---|---|
| Date | |
| Tracking No. | |
| Date Received | |

## NOTES

# ORDER

Order No.

Date

## CUSTOMER INFORMATION

| | | |
|---|---|---|
| Name | | Address |
| Company | | |
| Phone No. | | |
| Email | | |

## ORDER DETAILS

| No. | Item Description | QTY | Price | Discount | Total |
|---|---|---|---|---|---|
| | | | | | |
| | | | | | |
| | | | | | |
| | | | | | |
| | | | | | |
| | | | | | |
| | | | | | |
| | | | | | |
| | | | | | |
| | | | | | |
| | | | | | |
| | | | | | |

| | |
|---|---|
| Tax | |
| Shipping | |
| **TOTAL** | |

### ORDER STATUS

Started ☐     Completed ☐     Delivered ☐

## DELIVERY DETAILS

| | |
|---|---|
| Method | |
| Date | |
| Tracking No. | |
| Date Received | |

## NOTES

# ORDER

| Order No. | |
|---|---|
| Date | |

## CUSTOMER INFORMATION

| | | | |
|---|---|---|---|
| Name | | Address | |
| Company | | | |
| Phone No. | | | |
| Email | | | |

## ORDER DETAILS

| No. | Item Description | QTY | Price | Discount | Total |
|---|---|---|---|---|---|
| | | | | | |
| | | | | | |
| | | | | | |
| | | | | | |
| | | | | | |
| | | | | | |
| | | | | | |
| | | | | | |
| | | | | | |
| | | | | | |
| | | | | Tax | |
| | | | | Shipping | |

### ORDER STATUS

| Started ☐ | Completed ☐ | Delivered ☐ | **TOTAL** | |

## DELIVERY DETAILS

| Method | |
|---|---|
| Date | |
| Tracking No. | |
| Date Received | |

## NOTES

# ORDER

**Order No.**

**Date**

## CUSTOMER INFORMATION

| | |
|---|---|
| Name | |
| Company | |
| Phone No. | |
| Email | |

Address

## ORDER DETAILS

| No. | Item Description | QTY | Price | Discount | Total |
|---|---|---|---|---|---|
| | | | | | |
| | | | | | |
| | | | | | |
| | | | | | |
| | | | | | |
| | | | | | |
| | | | | | |
| | | | | | |
| | | | | | |
| | | | | | |

| | |
|---|---|
| Tax | |
| Shipping | |
| **TOTAL** | |

## ORDER STATUS

Started ☐     Completed ☐     Delivered ☐

## DELIVERY DETAILS

| | |
|---|---|
| Method | |
| Date | |
| Tracking No. | |
| Date Received | |

## NOTES

# ORDER

| Order No. | |
| --- | --- |
| Date | |

## CUSTOMER INFORMATION

| Name | | Address | |
| --- | --- | --- | --- |
| Company | | | |
| Phone No. | | | |
| Email | | | |

## ORDER DETAILS

| No. | Item Description | QTY | Price | Discount | Total |
| --- | --- | --- | --- | --- | --- |
| | | | | | |
| | | | | | |
| | | | | | |
| | | | | | |
| | | | | | |
| | | | | | |
| | | | | | |
| | | | | | |
| | | | | | |
| | | | | | |
| | | | | | |

| | Tax | |
| --- | --- | --- |
| | Shipping | |
| | **TOTAL** | |

### ORDER STATUS

Started ☐   Completed ☐   Delivered ☐

### DELIVERY DETAILS

| Method | |
| --- | --- |
| Date | |
| Tracking No. | |
| Date Received | |

### NOTES

# ORDER

Order No.

Date

## CUSTOMER INFORMATION

| Name | | Address | |
|---|---|---|---|
| Company | | | |
| Phone No. | | | |
| Email | | | |

## ORDER DETAILS

| No. | Item Description | QTY | Price | Discount | Total |
|---|---|---|---|---|---|
| | | | | | |
| | | | | | |
| | | | | | |
| | | | | | |
| | | | | | |
| | | | | | |
| | | | | | |
| | | | | | |
| | | | | | |
| | | | | | |
| | | | | Tax | |
| | | | | Shipping | |

## ORDER STATUS

Started ☐     Completed ☐     Delivered ☐

**TOTAL**

## DELIVERY DETAILS

| Method | |
|---|---|
| Date | |
| Tracking No. | |
| Date Received | |

## NOTES

# ORDER

| Order No. | |
|---|---|
| Date | |

## CUSTOMER INFORMATION

| Name | | Address | |
|---|---|---|---|
| Company | | | |
| Phone No. | | | |
| Email | | | |

## ORDER DETAILS

| No. | Item Description | QTY | Price | Discount | Total |
|---|---|---|---|---|---|
| | | | | | |
| | | | | | |
| | | | | | |
| | | | | | |
| | | | | | |
| | | | | | |
| | | | | | |
| | | | | | |
| | | | | | |
| | | | | | |
| | | | | | |

| | | |
|---|---|---|
| | Tax | |
| | Shipping | |
| | **TOTAL** | |

## ORDER STATUS

Started ☐     Completed ☐     Delivered ☐

## DELIVERY DETAILS

| Method | |
|---|---|
| Date | |
| Tracking No. | |
| Date Received | |

## NOTES

# ORDER

| Order No. | |
|---|---|
| Date | |

## CUSTOMER INFORMATION

| Name | |
|---|---|
| Company | |
| Phone No. | |
| Email | |

Address

## ORDER DETAILS

| No. | Item Description | QTY | Price | Discount | Total |
|---|---|---|---|---|---|
| | | | | | |
| | | | | | |
| | | | | | |
| | | | | | |
| | | | | | |
| | | | | | |
| | | | | | |
| | | | | | |
| | | | | | |
| | | | | | |
| | | | | | |

## ORDER STATUS

Started ☐  Completed ☐  Delivered ☐

| Tax | |
|---|---|
| Shipping | |
| **TOTAL** | |

## DELIVERY DETAILS

| Method | |
|---|---|
| Date | |
| Tracking No. | |
| Date Received | |

## NOTES

# ORDER

| Order No. | |
| --- | --- |
| Date | |

## CUSTOMER INFORMATION

| Name | |
| --- | --- |
| Company | |
| Phone No. | |
| Email | |

| Address | |
| --- | --- |
| | |

## ORDER DETAILS

| No. | Item Description | QTY | Price | Discount | Total |
| --- | --- | --- | --- | --- | --- |
| | | | | | |
| | | | | | |
| | | | | | |
| | | | | | |
| | | | | | |
| | | | | | |
| | | | | | |
| | | | | | |
| | | | | | |
| | | | | | |
| | | | | | |

| | |
| --- | --- |
| Tax | |
| Shiping | |
| **TOTAL** | |

## ORDER STATUS

Started ☐   Completed ☐   Delivered ☐

## DELIVERY DETAILS

| Method | |
| --- | --- |
| Date | |
| Tracking No. | |
| Date Received | |

## NOTES

# ORDER

| Order No. | |
| --- | --- |
| Date | |

## CUSTOMER INFORMATION

| Name | | Address | |
| --- | --- | --- | --- |
| Company | | | |
| Phone No. | | | |
| Email | | | |

## ORDER DETAILS

| No. | Item Description | QTY | Price | Discount | Total |
| --- | --- | --- | --- | --- | --- |
| | | | | | |
| | | | | | |
| | | | | | |
| | | | | | |
| | | | | | |
| | | | | | |
| | | | | | |
| | | | | | |
| | | | | | |
| | | | | | |
| | | | | | |

## ORDER STATUS

| Started ☐ | Completed ☐ | Delivered ☐ |
| --- | --- | --- |

| Tax | |
| --- | --- |
| Shipping | |
| **TOTAL** | |

## DELVERY DETAILS

| Method | |
| --- | --- |
| Date | |
| Tracking No. | |
| Date Received | |

## NOTES

# ORDER

| Order No. | |
|---|---|
| Date | |

## CUSTOMER INFORMATION

| Name | | Address | |
|---|---|---|---|
| Company | | | |
| Phone No. | | | |
| Email | | | |

## ORDER DETAILS

| No. | Item Description | QTY | Price | Discount | Total |
|---|---|---|---|---|---|
| | | | | | |
| | | | | | |
| | | | | | |
| | | | | | |
| | | | | | |
| | | | | | |
| | | | | | |
| | | | | | |
| | | | | | |
| | | | | | |
| | | | | | |

## ORDER STATUS

Started ☐    Completed ☐    Delivered ☐

| Tax | |
|---|---|
| Shipping | |
| **TOTAL** | |

## DELIVERY DETAILS

| Method | |
|---|---|
| Date | |
| Tracking No. | |
| Date Received | |

## NOTES

# ORDER

| Order No. | |
|---|---|
| Date | |

## CUSTOMER INFORMATION

| Name | | Address | |
|---|---|---|---|
| Company | | | |
| Phone No. | | | |
| Email | | | |

## ORDER DETAILS

| No. | Item Description | QTY | Price | Discount | Total |
|---|---|---|---|---|---|
| | | | | | |
| | | | | | |
| | | | | | |
| | | | | | |
| | | | | | |
| | | | | | |
| | | | | | |
| | | | | | |
| | | | | | |
| | | | | | |
| | | | | | |

| | Tax | |
|---|---|---|
| | Shipping | |
| | **TOTAL** | |

## ORDER STATUS

Started ☐   Completed ☐   Delivered ☐

## DELIVERY DETAILS

| Method | |
|---|---|
| Date | |
| Tracking No. | |
| Date Received | |

## NOTES

# ORDER

Order No.

Date

## CUSTOMER INFORMATION

| | |
|---|---|
| Name | |
| Company | |
| Phone No. | |
| Email | |

Address

## ORDER DETAILS

| No. | Item Description | QTY | Price | Discount | Total |
|---|---|---|---|---|---|
| | | | | | |
| | | | | | |
| | | | | | |
| | | | | | |
| | | | | | |
| | | | | | |
| | | | | | |
| | | | | | |
| | | | | | |
| | | | | | |
| | | | | | |

## ORDER STATUS

Started ☐      Completed ☐      Delivered ☐

| | |
|---|---|
| Tax | |
| Shipping | |
| **TOTAL** | |

## DELIVERY DETAILS

| | |
|---|---|
| Method | |
| Date | |
| Tracking No. | |
| Date Received | |

## NOTES

# ORDER

Order No.

Date

## CUSTOMER INFORMATION

| Name | | Address | |
| --- | --- | --- | --- |
| Company | | | |
| Phone No. | | | |
| Email | | | |

## ORDER DETAILS

| No. | Item Description | QTY | Price | Discount | Total |
| --- | --- | --- | --- | --- | --- |
| | | | | | |
| | | | | | |
| | | | | | |
| | | | | | |
| | | | | | |
| | | | | | |
| | | | | | |
| | | | | | |
| | | | | | |
| | | | | | |
| | | | | Tax | |
| | | | | Shipping | |
| | | | | **TOTAL** | |

## ORDER STATUS

Started ☐     Completed ☐     Delivered ☐

## DELIVERY DETAILS

| Method | |
| --- | --- |
| Date | |
| Tracking No. | |
| Date Received | |

## NOTES

# ORDER

| Order No. | |
| Date | |

## CUSTOMER INFORMATION

| Name | | Address | |
| Company | | | |
| Phone No. | | | |
| Email | | | |

## ORDER DETAILS

| No. | Item Description | QTY | Price | Discount | Total |
|---|---|---|---|---|---|
| | | | | | |
| | | | | | |
| | | | | | |
| | | | | | |
| | | | | | |
| | | | | | |
| | | | | | |
| | | | | | |
| | | | | | |
| | | | | | |
| | | | | | |

## ORDER STATUS

Started ☐    Completed ☐    Delivered ☐

| Tax | |
| Shipping | |
| **TOTAL** | |

## DELIVERY DETAILS

| Method | |
| Date | |
| Tracking No. | |
| Date Received | |

## NOTES

# ORDER

| | |
|---|---|
| Order No. | |
| Date | |

## CUSTOMER INFORMATION

| | |
|---|---|
| Name | |
| Company | |
| Phone No. | |
| Email | |

Address

## ORDER DETAILS

| No. | Item Description | QTY | Price | Discount | Total |
|---|---|---|---|---|---|
| | | | | | |
| | | | | | |
| | | | | | |
| | | | | | |
| | | | | | |
| | | | | | |
| | | | | | |
| | | | | | |
| | | | | | |
| | | | | | |
| | | | | | |
| | | | | | |

## ORDER STATUS

Started ☐   Completed ☐   Delivered ☐

| | |
|---|---|
| Tax | |
| Shipping | |
| **TOTAL** | |

## DELIVERY DETAILS

| | |
|---|---|
| Method | |
| Date | |
| Tracking No. | |
| Date Received | |

## NOTES

# ORDER

**Order No.**

**Date**

## CUSTOMER INFORMATION

| Name | | Address | |
|---|---|---|---|
| Company | | | |
| Phone No. | | | |
| Email | | | |

## ORDER DETAILS

| No. | Item Description | QTY | Price | Discount | Total |
|---|---|---|---|---|---|
| | | | | | |
| | | | | | |
| | | | | | |
| | | | | | |
| | | | | | |
| | | | | | |
| | | | | | |
| | | | | | |
| | | | | | |
| | | | | | |
| | | | | | |

| | Tax | |
|---|---|---|
| | Shipping | |
| | **TOTAL** | |

## ORDER STATUS

Started ☐    Completed ☐    Delivered ☐

## DELIVERY DETAILS

| Method | |
|---|---|
| Date | |
| Tracking No. | |
| Date Received | |

## NOTES

# ORDER

| Order No. | |
| Date | |

## CUSTOMER INFORMATION

| Name | | Address | |
| Company | | | |
| Phone No. | | | |
| Email | | | |

## ORDER DETAILS

| No. | Item Description | QTY | Price | Discount | Total |
|---|---|---|---|---|---|
| | | | | | |
| | | | | | |
| | | | | | |
| | | | | | |
| | | | | | |
| | | | | | |
| | | | | | |
| | | | | | |
| | | | | | |
| | | | | | |
| | | | | | |
| | | | | | |

| ORDER STATUS | Tax | |
| | Shipping | |
| Started ☐  Completed ☐  Delivered ☐ | **TOTAL** | |

## DELIVERY DETAILS

| Method | |
| Date | |
| Tracking No. | |
| Date Received | |

## NOTES

# ORDER

| Order No. | |
| Date | |

## CUSTOMER INFORMATION

| Name | |
|---|---|
| Company | |
| Phone No. | |
| Email | |

| Address | |
|---|---|
| | |

## ORDER DETAILS

| No. | Item Description | QTY | Price | Discount | Total |
|---|---|---|---|---|---|
| | | | | | |
| | | | | | |
| | | | | | |
| | | | | | |
| | | | | | |
| | | | | | |
| | | | | | |
| | | | | | |
| | | | | | |
| | | | | | |
| | | | | | |
| | | | | | |

## ORDER STATUS

Started ☐    Completed ☐    Delivered ☐

| Tax | |
|---|---|
| Shipping | |
| **TOTAL** | |

## DELIVERY DETAILS

| Method | |
|---|---|
| Date | |
| Tracking No. | |
| Date Received | |

## NOTES

# ORDER

| Order No. | |
| Date | |

## CUSTOMER INFORMATION

| Name | |
|---|---|
| Company | |
| Phone No. | |
| Email | |

| Address | |
|---|---|

## ORDER DETAILS

| No. | Item Description | QTY | Price | Discount | Total |
|---|---|---|---|---|---|
| | | | | | |
| | | | | | |
| | | | | | |
| | | | | | |
| | | | | | |
| | | | | | |
| | | | | | |
| | | | | | |
| | | | | | |
| | | | | | |
| | | | | | |

## ORDER STATUS

Started ☐  Completed ☐  Delivered ☐

| Tax | |
|---|---|
| Shipping | |
| **TOTAL** | |

## DELIVERY DETAILS

| Method | |
|---|---|
| Date | |
| Tracking No. | |
| Date Received | |

## NOTES

# ORDER

| Order No. | |
| Date | |

## CUSTOMER INFORMATION

| Name | |
|---|---|
| Company | |
| Phone No. | |
| Email | |

| Address | |
|---|---|

## ORDER DETAILS

| No. | Item Description | QTY | Price | Discount | Total |
|---|---|---|---|---|---|
| | | | | | |
| | | | | | |
| | | | | | |
| | | | | | |
| | | | | | |
| | | | | | |
| | | | | | |
| | | | | | |
| | | | | | |
| | | | | | |
| | | | | | |

## ORDER STATUS

Started ☐   Completed ☐   Delivered ☐

| Tax | |
|---|---|
| Shipping | |
| **TOTAL** | |

## DELIVERY DETAILS

| Method | |
|---|---|
| Date | |
| Tracking No. | |
| Date Received | |

## NOTES

# ORDER

| Order No. | |
| Date | |

## CUSTOMER INFORMATION

| Name | | Address | |
| Company | | | |
| Phone No. | | | |
| Email | | | |

## ORDER DETAILS

| No. | Item Description | QTY | Price | Discount | Total |
|-----|------------------|-----|-------|----------|-------|
|     |                  |     |       |          |       |
|     |                  |     |       |          |       |
|     |                  |     |       |          |       |
|     |                  |     |       |          |       |
|     |                  |     |       |          |       |
|     |                  |     |       |          |       |
|     |                  |     |       |          |       |
|     |                  |     |       |          |       |
|     |                  |     |       |          |       |
|     |                  |     |       |          |       |
|     |                  |     |       |          |       |

| Tax | |
| Shipping | |
| **TOTAL** | |

## ORDER STATUS

Started ☐    Completed ☐    Delivered ☐

## DELIVERY DETAILS

| Method | |
| Date | |
| Tracking No. | |
| Date Received | |

## NOTES

# ORDER

| Order No. | |
| Date | |

## CUSTOMER INFORMATION

| Name | | Address | |
| Company | | | |
| Phone No. | | | |
| Email | | | |

## ORDER DETAILS

| No. | Item Description | QTY | Price | Discount | Total |
|-----|------------------|-----|-------|----------|-------|
|  |  |  |  |  |  |
|  |  |  |  |  |  |
|  |  |  |  |  |  |
|  |  |  |  |  |  |
|  |  |  |  |  |  |
|  |  |  |  |  |  |
|  |  |  |  |  |  |
|  |  |  |  |  |  |
|  |  |  |  |  |  |
|  |  |  |  |  |  |
|  |  |  |  |  |  |
|  |  |  |  |  |  |
|  |  |  |  | Tax |  |
|  |  |  |  | Shipping |  |
|  |  |  |  | **TOTAL** |  |

## ORDER STATUS

Started ☐     Completed ☐     Delivered ☐

## DELIVERY DETAILS

| Method | |
| Date | |
| Tracking No. | |
| Date Received | |

## NOTES

# ORDER

| Order No. | |
|---|---|
| Date | |

## CUSTOMER INFORMATION

| Name | | Address | |
|---|---|---|---|
| Company | | | |
| Phone No. | | | |
| Email | | | |

## ORDER DETAILS

| No. | Item Description | QTY | Price | Discount | Total |
|---|---|---|---|---|---|
| | | | | | |
| | | | | | |
| | | | | | |
| | | | | | |
| | | | | | |
| | | | | | |
| | | | | | |
| | | | | | |
| | | | | | |
| | | | | | |
| | | | | | |
| | | | | Tax | |
| | | | | Shipping | |

## ORDER STATUS

Started ☐    Completed ☐    Delivered ☐

**TOTAL**

## DELIVERY DETAILS

| Method | |
|---|---|
| Date | |
| Tracking No. | |
| Date Received | |

## NOTES

# ORDER

| Order No. | |
|---|---|
| Date | |

## CUSTOMER INFORMATION

| Name | |
|---|---|
| Company | |
| Phone No. | |
| Email | |

Address

## ORDER DETAILS

| No. | Item Description | QTY | Price | Discount | Total |
|---|---|---|---|---|---|
| | | | | | |
| | | | | | |
| | | | | | |
| | | | | | |
| | | | | | |
| | | | | | |
| | | | | | |
| | | | | | |
| | | | | | |
| | | | | | |
| | | | | | |

| | Tax | |
|---|---|---|
| | Shipping | |
| | **TOTAL** | |

## ORDER STATUS

Started ☐   Completed ☐   Delivered ☐

## DELIVERY DETAILS

| Method | |
|---|---|
| Date | |
| Tracking No. | |
| Date Received | |

## NOTES

# ORDER

| Order No. | |
| Date | |

## CUSTOMER INFORMATION

| Name | |
| Company | |
| Phone No. | |
| Email | |

| Address | |

## ORDER DETAILS

| No. | Item Description | QTY | Price | Discount | Total |
|---|---|---|---|---|---|
| | | | | | |
| | | | | | |
| | | | | | |
| | | | | | |
| | | | | | |
| | | | | | |
| | | | | | |
| | | | | | |
| | | | | | |
| | | | | | |
| | | | | | |
| | | | | | |

| | Tax | |
| | Shipping | |

## ORDER STATUS

Started ☐    Completed ☐    Delivered ☐

| TOTAL | |

## DELIVERY DETAILS

| Method | |
| Date | |
| Tracking No. | |
| Date Received | |

## NOTES

# ORDER

| Order No. | |
|---|---|
| Date | |

## CUSTOMER INFORMATION

| Name | | Address | |
|---|---|---|---|
| Company | | | |
| Phone No. | | | |
| Email | | | |

## ORDER DETAILS

| No. | Item Description | QTY | Price | Discount | Total |
|---|---|---|---|---|---|
| | | | | | |
| | | | | | |
| | | | | | |
| | | | | | |
| | | | | | |
| | | | | | |
| | | | | | |
| | | | | | |
| | | | | | |
| | | | | | |
| | | | | | |
| | | | | Tax | |
| | | | | Shipping | |

## ORDER STATUS

Started ☐   Completed ☐   Delivered ☐

**TOTAL**

## DELIVERY DETAILS

| Method | |
|---|---|
| Date | |
| Tracking No. | |
| Date Received | |

## NOTES

# ORDER

Order No.

Date

## CUSTOMER INFORMATION

| Name | |
|---|---|
| Company | |
| Phone No. | |
| Email | |

Address

## ORDER DETAILS

| No. | Item Description | QTY | Price | Discount | Total |
|---|---|---|---|---|---|
| | | | | | |
| | | | | | |
| | | | | | |
| | | | | | |
| | | | | | |
| | | | | | |
| | | | | | |
| | | | | | |
| | | | | | |
| | | | | | |
| | | | | | |

## ORDER STATUS

Started ☐     Completed ☐     Delivered ☐

Tax

Shipping

**TOTAL**

## DELIVERY DETAILS

| Method | |
|---|---|
| Date | |
| Tracking No. | |
| Date Received | |

## NOTES

# ORDER

| Order No. | |
| Date | |

## CUSTOMER INFORMATION

| Name | |
| Company | |
| Phone No. | |
| Email | |

| Address | |

## ORDER DETAILS

| No. | Item Description | QTY | Price | Discount | Total |
|---|---|---|---|---|---|
| | | | | | |
| | | | | | |
| | | | | | |
| | | | | | |
| | | | | | |
| | | | | | |
| | | | | | |
| | | | | | |
| | | | | | |
| | | | | | |
| | | | | | |

| | Tax | |
|---|---|---|
| | Shipping | |
| | **TOTAL** | |

## ORDER STATUS

Started ☐     Completed ☐     Delivered ☐

## DELIVERY DETAILS

| Method | |
| Date | |
| Tracking No. | |
| Date Received | |

## NOTES

# ORDER

| Order No. | |
|---|---|
| Date | |

## CUSTOMER INFORMATION

| Name | | Address | |
|---|---|---|---|
| Company | | | |
| Phone No. | | | |
| Email | | | |

## ORDER DETAILS

| No. | Item Description | QTY | Price | Discount | Total |
|---|---|---|---|---|---|
| | | | | | |
| | | | | | |
| | | | | | |
| | | | | | |
| | | | | | |
| | | | | | |
| | | | | | |
| | | | | | |
| | | | | | |
| | | | | | |

| | Tax | |
|---|---|---|
| | Shipping | |

## ORDER STATUS

Started ☐    Completed ☐    Delivered ☐

**TOTAL**

## DELIVERY DETAILS

| Method | |
|---|---|
| Date | |
| Tracking No. | |
| Date Received | |

## NOTES

# ORDER

| Order No. | |
| Date | |

## CUSTOMER INFORMATION

| Name | | Address | |
|---|---|---|---|
| Company | | | |
| Phone No. | | | |
| Email | | | |

## ORDER DETAILS

| No. | Item Description | QTY | Price | Discount | Total |
|---|---|---|---|---|---|
| | | | | | |
| | | | | | |
| | | | | | |
| | | | | | |
| | | | | | |
| | | | | | |
| | | | | | |
| | | | | | |
| | | | | | |
| | | | | | |
| | | | | | |
| | | | | Tax | |
| | | | | Shipping | |
| | | | | **TOTAL** | |

## ORDER STATUS

Started ☐   Completed ☐   Delivered ☐

## DELIVERY DETAILS

| Method | |
|---|---|
| Date | |
| Tracking No. | |
| Date Received | |

## NOTES

# ORDER

| Order No. | |
|---|---|
| Date | |

## CUSTOMER INFORMATION

| Name | |
|---|---|
| Company | |
| Phone No. | |
| Email | |

Address

## ORDER DETAILS

| No. | Item Description | QTY | Price | Discount | Total |
|---|---|---|---|---|---|
| | | | | | |
| | | | | | |
| | | | | | |
| | | | | | |
| | | | | | |
| | | | | | |
| | | | | | |
| | | | | | |
| | | | | | |
| | | | | | |

## ORDER STATUS

Started ☐    Completed ☐    Delivered ☐

| Tax | |
|---|---|
| Shipping | |
| **TOTAL** | |

## DELIVERY DETAILS

| Method | |
|---|---|
| Date | |
| Tracking No. | |
| Date Received | |

## NOTES

# ORDER

| Order No. | |
| Date | |

## CUSTOMER INFORMATION

| Name | |
| Company | |
| Phone No. | |
| Email | |

Address:

## ORDER DETAILS

| No. | Item Description | QTY | Price | Discount | Total |
|---|---|---|---|---|---|
| | | | | | |
| | | | | | |
| | | | | | |
| | | | | | |
| | | | | | |
| | | | | | |
| | | | | | |
| | | | | | |
| | | | | | |
| | | | | | |

## ORDER STATUS

Started ☐   Completed ☐   Delivered ☐

| Tax | |
| Shipping | |
| **TOTAL** | |

## DELIVERY DETAILS

| Method | |
| Date | |
| Tracking No. | |
| Date Received | |

## NOTES

# ORDER

**Order No.**

**Date**

## CUSTOMER INFORMATION

| | |
|---|---|
| Name | |
| Company | |
| Phone No. | |
| Email | |

Address

## ORDER DETAILS

| No. | Item Description | QTY | Price | Discount | Total |
|---|---|---|---|---|---|
| | | | | | |
| | | | | | |
| | | | | | |
| | | | | | |
| | | | | | |
| | | | | | |
| | | | | | |
| | | | | | |
| | | | | | |
| | | | | | |
| | | | | | |

Tax

Shipping

**TOTAL**

## ORDER STATUS

Started ☐   Completed ☐   Delivered ☐

## DELIVERY DETAILS

| | |
|---|---|
| Method | |
| Date | |
| Tracking No. | |
| Date Received | |

## NOTES

# ORDER

| Order No. | |
| Date | |

## CUSTOMER INFORMATION

| Name | |
| Company | |
| Phone No. | |
| Email | |

| Address | |

## ORDER DETAILS

| No. | Item Description | QTY | Price | Discount | Total |
|---|---|---|---|---|---|
| | | | | | |
| | | | | | |
| | | | | | |
| | | | | | |
| | | | | | |
| | | | | | |
| | | | | | |
| | | | | | |
| | | | | | |
| | | | | | |
| | | | | | |

| | |
|---|---|
| Tax | |
| Shipping | |
| **TOTAL** | |

## ORDER STATUS

Started ☐    Completed ☐    Delivered ☐

## DELIVERY DETAILS

| Method | |
| Date | |
| Tracking No. | |
| Date Received | |

## NOTES

# ORDER

| Order No. | |
|---|---|
| Date | |

## CUSTOMER INFORMATION

| Name | | Address | |
|---|---|---|---|
| Company | | | |
| Phone No. | | | |
| Email | | | |

## ORDER DETAILS

| No. | Item Description | QTY | Price | Discount | Total |
|---|---|---|---|---|---|
| | | | | | |
| | | | | | |
| | | | | | |
| | | | | | |
| | | | | | |
| | | | | | |
| | | | | | |
| | | | | | |
| | | | | | |
| | | | | | |

| | | |
|---|---|---|
| | Tax | |
| | Shipping | |
| | **TOTAL** | |

## ORDER STATUS

Started ☐    Completed ☐    Delivered ☐

## DELIVERY DETAILS

| Method | |
|---|---|
| Date | |
| Tracking No. | |
| Date Received | |

## NOTES

# ORDER

| | |
|---|---|
| Order No. | |
| Date | |

## CUSTOMER INFORMATION

| | | | |
|---|---|---|---|
| Name | | Address | |
| Company | | | |
| Phone No. | | | |
| Email | | | |

## ORDER DETAILS

| No. | Item Description | QTY | Price | Discount | Total |
|---|---|---|---|---|---|
| | | | | | |
| | | | | | |
| | | | | | |
| | | | | | |
| | | | | | |
| | | | | | |
| | | | | | |
| | | | | | |
| | | | | | |
| | | | | | |
| | | | | | |
| | | | Tax | | |
| | | | Shipping | | |
| | | | **TOTAL** | | |

## ORDER STATUS

Started ☐     Completed ☐     Delivered ☐

## DELIVERY DETAILS

| | |
|---|---|
| Method | |
| Date | |
| Tracking No. | |
| Date Received | |

## NOTES

# ORDER

| | |
|---|---|
| Order No. | |
| Date | |

## CUSTOMER INFORMATION

| | | | |
|---|---|---|---|
| Name | | Address | |
| Company | | | |
| Phone No. | | | |
| Email | | | |

## ORDER DETAILS

| No. | Item Description | QTY | Price | Discount | Total |
|---|---|---|---|---|---|
| | | | | | |
| | | | | | |
| | | | | | |
| | | | | | |
| | | | | | |
| | | | | | |
| | | | | | |
| | | | | | |
| | | | | | |
| | | | | | |
| | | | | | |
| | | | | Tax | |
| | | | | Shipping | |

## ORDER STATUS

Started ☐     Completed ☐     Delivered ☐

**TOTAL**

## DELIVERY DETAILS

| | |
|---|---|
| Method | |
| Date | |
| Tracking No. | |
| Date Received | |

## NOTES

# ORDER

| Order No. | |
|---|---|
| Date | |

## CUSTOMER INFORMATION

| Name | | Address | |
|---|---|---|---|
| Company | | | |
| Phone No. | | | |
| Email | | | |

## ORDER DETAILS

| No. | Item Description | QTY | Price | Discount | Total |
|---|---|---|---|---|---|
| | | | | | |
| | | | | | |
| | | | | | |
| | | | | | |
| | | | | | |
| | | | | | |
| | | | | | |
| | | | | | |
| | | | | | |
| | | | | | |

## ORDER STATUS

Started ☐   Completed ☐   Delivered ☐

| Tax | |
|---|---|
| Shipping | |
| **TOTAL** | |

## DELIVERY DETAILS

| Method | |
|---|---|
| Date | |
| Tracking No. | |
| Date Received | |

## NOTES

# ORDER

**Order No.**

**Date**

## CUSTOMER INFORMATION

| Name | | Address | |
|---|---|---|---|
| Company | | | |
| Phone No. | | | |
| Email | | | |

## ORDER DETAILS

| No. | Item Description | QTY | Price | Discount | Total |
|---|---|---|---|---|---|
| | | | | | |
| | | | | | |
| | | | | | |
| | | | | | |
| | | | | | |
| | | | | | |
| | | | | | |
| | | | | | |
| | | | | | |
| | | | | | |

## ORDER STATUS

Started ☐    Completed ☐    Delivered ☐

| Tax | |
|---|---|
| Shipping | |
| **TOTAL** | |

## DELIVERY DETAILS

| Method | |
|---|---|
| Date | |
| Tracking No. | |
| Date Received | |

## NOTES

# ORDER

| Order No. | |
| Date | |

## CUSTOMER INFORMATION

| Name | | Address | |
| Company | | | |
| Phone No. | | | |
| Email | | | |

## ORDER DETAILS

| No. | Item Description | QTY | Price | Discount | Total |
|---|---|---|---|---|---|
| | | | | | |
| | | | | | |
| | | | | | |
| | | | | | |
| | | | | | |
| | | | | | |
| | | | | | |
| | | | | | |
| | | | | | |
| | | | | | |
| | | | | | |
| | | | | Tax | |
| | | | | Shipping | |

## ORDER STATUS

Started ☐     Completed ☐     Delivered ☐     **TOTAL**

## DELIVERY DETAILS

| Method | |
| Date | |
| Tracking No. | |
| Date Received | |

## NOTES

# ORDER

**Order No.**

**Date**

## CUSTOMER INFORMATION

| | | Address |
|---|---|---|
| Name | | |
| Company | | |
| Phone No. | | |
| Email | | |

## ORDER DETAILS

| No. | Item Description | QTY | Price | Discount | Total |
|---|---|---|---|---|---|
| | | | | | |
| | | | | | |
| | | | | | |
| | | | | | |
| | | | | | |
| | | | | | |
| | | | | | |
| | | | | | |
| | | | | | |
| | | | | | |

| | Tax | |
|---|---|---|
| | Shipping | |
| | **TOTAL** | |

## ORDER STATUS

Started ☐    Completed ☐    Delivered ☐

## DELIVERY DETAILS

| Method | |
|---|---|
| Date | |
| Tracking No. | |
| Date Received | |

## NOTES

# ORDER

| Order No. | |
|---|---|
| Date | |

## CUSTOMER INFORMATION

| | | Address | |
|---|---|---|---|
| Name | | | |
| Company | | | |
| Phone No. | | | |
| Email | | | |

## ORDER DETAILS

| No. | Item Description | QTY | Price | Discount | Total |
|---|---|---|---|---|---|
| | | | | | |
| | | | | | |
| | | | | | |
| | | | | | |
| | | | | | |
| | | | | | |
| | | | | | |
| | | | | | |
| | | | | | |
| | | | | | |
| | | | | | |

## ORDER STATUS

| | Tax | |
|---|---|---|
| | Shipping | |
| Started ☐   Completed ☐   Delivered ☐ | **TOTAL** | |

## DELIVERY DETAILS

| Method | |
|---|---|
| Date | |
| Tracking No. | |
| Date Received | |

## NOTES

# ORDER

| Order No. | |
|---|---|
| Date | |

## CUSTOMER INFORMATION

| Name | |
|---|---|
| Company | |
| Phone No. | |
| Email | |

Address

## ORDER DETAILS

| No. | Item Description | QTY | Price | Discount | Total |
|---|---|---|---|---|---|
| | | | | | |
| | | | | | |
| | | | | | |
| | | | | | |
| | | | | | |
| | | | | | |
| | | | | | |
| | | | | | |
| | | | | | |
| | | | | | |
| | | | | | |

| | Tax | |
|---|---|---|
| | Shipping | |
| | **TOTAL** | |

## ORDER STATUS

Started ☐    Completed ☐    Delivered ☐

## DELIVERY DETAILS

| Method | |
|---|---|
| Date | |
| Tracking No. | |
| Date Received | |

## NOTES

# ORDER

| Order No. | |
| Date | |

## CUSTOMER INFORMATION

| Name | | Address | |
| Company | | | |
| Phone No. | | | |
| Email | | | |

## ORDER DETAILS

| No. | Item Description | QTY | Price | Discount | Total |
|-----|------------------|-----|-------|----------|-------|
|     |                  |     |       |          |       |
|     |                  |     |       |          |       |
|     |                  |     |       |          |       |
|     |                  |     |       |          |       |
|     |                  |     |       |          |       |
|     |                  |     |       |          |       |
|     |                  |     |       |          |       |
|     |                  |     |       |          |       |
|     |                  |     |       |          |       |
|     |                  |     |       |          |       |

| | Tax | |
| ORDER STATUS | Shipping | |

Started ☐    Completed ☐    Delivered ☐    **TOTAL**

## DELIVERY DETAILS

| Method | |
| Date | |
| Tracking No. | |
| Date Received | |

## NOTES

# ORDER

Order No.

Date

## CUSTOMER INFORMATION

| | |
|---|---|
| Name | |
| Company | |
| Phone No. | |
| Email | |

Address

## ORDER DETAILS

| No. | Item Description | QTY | Price | Discount | Total |
|---|---|---|---|---|---|
| | | | | | |
| | | | | | |
| | | | | | |
| | | | | | |
| | | | | | |
| | | | | | |
| | | | | | |
| | | | | | |
| | | | | | |
| | | | | | |
| | | | | | |

## ORDER STATUS

Started ☐   Completed ☐   Delivered ☐

Tax

Shipping

**TOTAL**

## DELIVERY DETAILS

| | |
|---|---|
| Method | |
| Date | |
| Tracking No. | |
| Date Received | |

## NOTES

# ORDER

| Order No. | |
|---|---|
| Date | |

## CUSTOMER INFORMATION

| Name | | Address | |
|---|---|---|---|
| Company | | | |
| Phone No. | | | |
| Email | | | |

## ORDER DETAILS

| No. | Item Description | QTY | Price | Discount | Total |
|---|---|---|---|---|---|
| | | | | | |
| | | | | | |
| | | | | | |
| | | | | | |
| | | | | | |
| | | | | | |
| | | | | | |
| | | | | | |
| | | | | | |
| | | | | | |

| | | |
|---|---|---|
| | Tax | |
| | Shipping | |

## ORDER STATUS

Started ☐    Completed ☐    Delivered ☐    **TOTAL**

## DELIVERY DETAILS

| Method | |
|---|---|
| Date | |
| Tracking No. | |
| Date Received | |

## NOTES

# ORDER

| Order No. | |
|---|---|
| Date | |

## CUSTOMER INFORMATION

| Name | | Address | |
|---|---|---|---|
| Company | | | |
| Phone No. | | | |
| Email | | | |

## ORDER DETAILS

| No. | Item Description | QTY | Price | Discount | Total |
|---|---|---|---|---|---|
| | | | | | |
| | | | | | |
| | | | | | |
| | | | | | |
| | | | | | |
| | | | | | |
| | | | | | |
| | | | | | |
| | | | | | |
| | | | | | |
| | | | | | |

## ORDER STATUS

Started ☐     Completed ☐     Delivered ☐

| Tax | |
|---|---|
| Shipping | |
| **TOTAL** | |

## DELIVERY DETAILS

| Method | |
|---|---|
| Date | |
| Tracking No. | |
| Date Received | |

## NOTES

# ORDER

| Order No. | |
|---|---|
| Date | |

## CUSTOMER INFORMATION

| Name | | Address | |
|---|---|---|---|
| Company | | | |
| Phone No. | | | |
| Email | | | |

## ORDER DETAILS

| No. | Item Description | QTY | Price | Discount | Total |
|---|---|---|---|---|---|
| | | | | | |
| | | | | | |
| | | | | | |
| | | | | | |
| | | | | | |
| | | | | | |
| | | | | | |
| | | | | | |
| | | | | | |
| | | | | | |
| | | | | | |
| | | | | | |

|  |  |  | Tax | |
|---|---|---|---|---|
| **ORDER STATUS** | | | Shipping | |
| Started ☐ | Completed ☐ | Delivered ☐ | **TOTAL** | |

## DELIVERY DETAILS

| Method | |
|---|---|
| Date | |
| Tracking No. | |
| Date Received | |

## NOTES

# ORDER

| Order No. | |
|---|---|
| Date | |

## CUSTOMER INFORMATION

| Name | | Address | |
|---|---|---|---|
| Company | | | |
| Phone No. | | | |
| Email | | | |

## ORDER DETAILS

| No. | Item Description | QTY | Price | Discount | Total |
|---|---|---|---|---|---|
| | | | | | |
| | | | | | |
| | | | | | |
| | | | | | |
| | | | | | |
| | | | | | |
| | | | | | |
| | | | | | |
| | | | | | |
| | | | | | |
| | | | | | |
| | | | | Tax | |
| | | | | Shipping | |

## ORDER STATUS

Started ☐  Completed ☐  Delivered ☐

**TOTAL**

## DELIVERY DETAILS

| Method | |
|---|---|
| Date | |
| Tracking No. | |
| Date Received | |

## NOTES

# ORDER

| Order No. | |
| Date | |

## CUSTOMER INFORMATION

| Name | | Address | |
| Company | | | |
| Phone No. | | | |
| Email | | | |

## ORDER DETAILS

| No. | Item Description | QTY | Price | Discount | Total |
|---|---|---|---|---|---|
| | | | | | |
| | | | | | |
| | | | | | |
| | | | | | |
| | | | | | |
| | | | | | |
| | | | | | |
| | | | | | |
| | | | | | |
| | | | | | |
| | | | | | |
| | | | | Tax | |
| | | | | Shipping | |
| | | | | **TOTAL** | |

## ORDER STATUS

Started ☐     Completed ☐     Delivered ☐

## DELIVERY DETAILS

| Method | |
| Date | |
| Tracking No. | |
| Date Received | |

## NOTES

# ORDER

| | |
|---|---|
| Order No. | |
| Date | |

## CUSTOMER INFORMATION

| | | | |
|---|---|---|---|
| Name | | Address | |
| Company | | | |
| Phone No. | | | |
| Email | | | |

## ORDER DETAILS

| No. | Item Description | QTY | Price | Discount | Total |
|---|---|---|---|---|---|
| | | | | | |
| | | | | | |
| | | | | | |
| | | | | | |
| | | | | | |
| | | | | | |
| | | | | | |
| | | | | | |
| | | | | | |
| | | | | | |
| | | | | | |

### ORDER STATUS

Started ☐   Completed ☐   Delivered ☐

| | |
|---|---|
| Tax | |
| Shipping | |
| **TOTAL** | |

## DELIVERY DETAILS

| | |
|---|---|
| Method | |
| Date | |
| Tracking No. | |
| Date Received | |

## NOTES

# ORDER

| Order No. | |
| --- | --- |
| Date | |

## CUSTOMER INFORMATION

| Name | | Address | |
| --- | --- | --- | --- |
| Company | | | |
| Phone No. | | | |
| Email | | | |

## ORDER DETAILS

| No. | Item Description | QTY | Price | Discount | Total |
| --- | --- | --- | --- | --- | --- |
| | | | | | |
| | | | | | |
| | | | | | |
| | | | | | |
| | | | | | |
| | | | | | |
| | | | | | |
| | | | | | |
| | | | | | |
| | | | | | |
| | | | | Tax | |
| | | | | Shipping | |

## ORDER STATUS

Started ☐    Completed ☐    Delivered ☐

**TOTAL**

## DELIVERY DETAILS

| Method | |
| --- | --- |
| Date | |
| Tracking No. | |
| Date Received | |

## NOTES

# ORDER

Order No.

Date

## CUSTOMER INFORMATION

| Name |  | Address |
|---|---|---|
| Company |  |  |
| Phone No. |  |  |
| Email |  |  |

## ORDER DETAILS

| No. | Item Description | QTY | Price | Discount | Total |
|---|---|---|---|---|---|
|  |  |  |  |  |  |
|  |  |  |  |  |  |
|  |  |  |  |  |  |
|  |  |  |  |  |  |
|  |  |  |  |  |  |
|  |  |  |  |  |  |
|  |  |  |  |  |  |
|  |  |  |  |  |  |
|  |  |  |  |  |  |
|  |  |  |  |  |  |
|  |  |  |  |  |  |

## ORDER STATUS

Started ☐    Completed ☐    Delivered ☐

Tax

Shipping

**TOTAL**

## DELIVERY DETAILS

| Method |  |
|---|---|
| Date |  |
| Tracking No. |  |
| Date Received |  |

## NOTES

# ORDER

| Order No. | |
| Date | |

## CUSTOMER INFORMATION

| Name | | Address | |
| Company | | | |
| Phone No. | | | |
| Email | | | |

## ORDER DETAILS

| No. | Item Description | QTY | Price | Discount | Total |
|---|---|---|---|---|---|
| | | | | | |
| | | | | | |
| | | | | | |
| | | | | | |
| | | | | | |
| | | | | | |
| | | | | | |
| | | | | | |
| | | | | | |
| | | | | | |
| | | | | | |

| | Tax | |
|---|---|---|
| | Shipping | |
| | **TOTAL** | |

## ORDER STATUS

Started ☐    Completed ☐    Delivered ☐

## DELIVERY DETAILS

| Method | |
| Date | |
| Tracking No. | |
| Date Received | |

## NOTES

# ORDER

| Order No. | |
| Date | |

## CUSTOMER INFORMATION

| Name | | Address | |
| Company | | | |
| Phone No. | | | |
| Email | | | |

## ORDER DETAILS

| No. | Item Description | QTY | Price | Discount | Total |
|-----|------------------|-----|-------|----------|-------|
|     |                  |     |       |          |       |
|     |                  |     |       |          |       |
|     |                  |     |       |          |       |
|     |                  |     |       |          |       |
|     |                  |     |       |          |       |
|     |                  |     |       |          |       |
|     |                  |     |       |          |       |
|     |                  |     |       |          |       |
|     |                  |     |       |          |       |
|     |                  |     |       |          |       |

| Tax | |
| Shipping | |
| **TOTAL** | |

## ORDER STATUS

Started ☐     Completed ☐     Delivered ☐

## DELIVERY DETAILS

| Method | |
| Date | |
| Tracking No. | |
| Date Received | |

## NOTES

# ORDER

Order No.

Date

## CUSTOMER INFORMATION

| Name | |
|---|---|
| Company | |
| Phone No. | |
| Email | |

Address

## ORDER DETAILS

| No. | Item Description | QTY | Price | Discount | Total |
|---|---|---|---|---|---|
| | | | | | |
| | | | | | |
| | | | | | |
| | | | | | |
| | | | | | |
| | | | | | |
| | | | | | |
| | | | | | |
| | | | | | |
| | | | | | |
| | | | | | |

## ORDER STATUS

Started ☐    Completed ☐    Delivered ☐

| Tax | |
|---|---|
| Shipping | |
| **TOTAL** | |

## DELIVERY DETAILS

| Method | |
|---|---|
| Date | |
| Tracking No. | |
| Date Received | |

## NOTES

# ORDER

| Order No. | |
|---|---|
| Date | |

## CUSTOMER INFORMATION

| Name | | Address | |
|---|---|---|---|
| Company | | | |
| Phone No. | | | |
| Email | | | |

## ORDER DETAILS

| No. | Item Description | QTY | Price | Discount | Total |
|---|---|---|---|---|---|
| | | | | | |
| | | | | | |
| | | | | | |
| | | | | | |
| | | | | | |
| | | | | | |
| | | | | | |
| | | | | | |
| | | | | | |
| | | | | | |

| ORDER STATUS | | | Tax | |
|---|---|---|---|---|
| | | | Shipping | |
| Started ☐ | Completed ☐ | Delivered ☐ | **TOTAL** | |

## DELIVERY DETAILS

| Method | |
|---|---|
| Date | |
| Tracking No. | |
| Date Received | |

## NOTES

# ORDER

| Order No. | |
|---|---|
| Date | |

## CUSTOMER INFORMATION

| | | | |
|---|---|---|---|
| Name | | Address | |
| Company | | | |
| Phone No. | | | |
| Email | | | |

## ORDER DETAILS

| No. | Item Description | QTY | Price | Discount | Total |
|---|---|---|---|---|---|
| | | | | | |
| | | | | | |
| | | | | | |
| | | | | | |
| | | | | | |
| | | | | | |
| | | | | | |
| | | | | | |
| | | | | | |
| | | | | | |
| | | | | Tax | |
| | | | | Shipping | |

## ORDER STATUS

Started ☐    Completed ☐    Delivered ☐    **TOTAL**

## DELIVERY DETAILS

| Method | |
|---|---|
| Date | |
| Tracking No. | |
| Date Received | |

## NOTES

CPSIA information can be obtained
at www.ICGtesting.com
Printed in the USA
LVHW101618230221
679614LV00008B/352